MW01241631

You're a PIMP How to avoid sexual HarASSment

Mr. G Hud

ISBN (9781701792463)

Dedication

For:

From :

(circle one)
Happy Birthday
Happy Anniversary
Congratulations
Happy Retirement
Merry Christmas
Happy Holidays
Divorce
You got a promotion
You no longer have Herpes
You Won the Lottery. Don't forget about me.
You got out of Prison

other_____

Preface

Just a silly book to have fun with. So roll with it.

This Book is for you

This is a G

Hud

Gag Gift

Book

THIS BOOK IS COMPLETELY USELESS. THERE IS NO USEFUL INFORMATION OF ANY KIND WITHIN THE PAGES YOU ARE ABOUT TO SKIM THROUGH. IT IS THE WORST BOOK YOU WILL EVER FIND ON THIS SUBJECT. THERE IS NO ADVENTURE, NO SUSPENSE, NO SEX, NO CLIFF HANGERS, NO ROMANCE, NO DRAMA. IT'S THE MOST PATHETIC BOOK YOU'LL EVER OWN.

FEEL FREE TO USE THE PAGES IN THIS BOOK FOR WHAT EVER YOU WANT TO DO WITH IT. USE IT AS A NOTEBOOK. RIP OUT THE PAGES AND MAKE PAPER AIRPLANES. DOODLE IN IT. HELL, IT'S YOUR BOOK SO DO WHAT EVER YOU WANT TO DO WITH IT. JUST DON'T SEND IT BACK TO ME. I DON'T WANT IT. I'VE ALREADY GOT ENOUGH STUFF LAYING AROUND.

FIND MY FACEBOOK PAGE

GREGORY HUDSON BOOKS

THERE ACTUALLY IS SOME SERIOUS TALENT THERE, REALLY. I'M SERIOUS

BLAH BLAH

BLAH…

_____

_____

_____

_____

_____

_____

BLAH

BLAH

_____

_____

_____

_____

_____

_____

_____

DOODLE TIME

WHAT DOES A COW SAY?

_____

_____

_____

_____

_____

_____

_____

WHAT TIME IS IT RIGHT NOW?

_____

_____

_____

_____

_____

_____

_____

_____

_____

_____

THIS IS THIS PAGE

WOW! Just WOW!!

_____

_____

_____

_____

_____

_____

_____

_____

_____

_____

I can't believe you are looking at this page

_____

_____

_____

_____

_____

_____

_____

_ Are we there yet?

_____

Dear Diary,

let's play a game?

_____

_____

_____

_____

_____

_____ Blah Blah Blah

_____

_____

_____

_____

Today's weather brought to you by God

_____

_____

_____

_____

_____

_____

_____

_____ Sitting here_____

again doing absolutely nothing

_____ Today's bowl

movement was more exciting than this book

_____

_____

_____

Excuse me while I ….. never mind

_____

_____

_____

_____

_____

_____

_____

_____

_____

Feel free to fill in the blanks

Today I feel like

_____

Tomorrow I will feel like

_____

Next week I plan to

_____

_____

_____

_____

__ I'm so tired of this crap

_____

_____

_____

_____

_____

_____

_____

Your signature is required

_____

_____

_____

_____

_____

_____

_____

_____

_____

_____

_____

_____

_____

_____

___ if animals could talk, which species

would be the rudest of them all?

_____

How many words can you make using these letters?-

ABCDEFGHIJKLMNOPQRSTUVWXYZ_

_____

_____

_____

_____

_____

_____

_____

_____

_____

_____

_____

_____

_____ What if all

the grass in the world was replaced with

potato sticks?

_____

_____

_____

_____

_____

_____

_____

_____

_____

_____

_____

_____

_____

_____

_____ Would you

rather own a horse the size of a cat or a cat

the size of a mouse?

_____

_____

_____

_____

_____

_____

_____

_____

_____

_____ Just think!!

___ More doodle space _____

_____ this

book really does suck

_____

_____

_____

_____

_____

_____

_____ Just think if your arms were

detachable

_____

_____

_____

_____

_____

_____

_____ Meanwhile, on a

planet far far away. _____

_____

_____

_____

_____

_____

_____

_____

_____

_____ I just can't even

_____

_____

_____

_____

_____

_____

_____

_____

_____

_____

_____

_____

_____

_____

_____

_____

_____H

ow many chickens would it take to kill a

lion? _____

_____

_____

_____

_____

_____

_____

_____

_____

_____

_____

_____

_____

_____

_____ your

words go here _____

What one super power do you wish to have? __

_____

_____

_____

_____

_____

_____

_____

_____

_____ questions, questions,

questions

_____

_____

_____

_____

_____

_____

_____ What is something that doesn't smell

good but you want to smell it anyway?

_____

_____

_____

_____

Do we need a president for the world wide web?

_____ Stop right

now, How many fingers are you holding up?

_____

_____

_____

_____

_____

_____

_____

_____

_____

_____ Are you wearing underwear today?

_____

_____

_____

_____

_____

Which would you rather give up for life,

Toilet paper or the internet?

_____

_____

_____

_____

_____

_____

_____

_____

_____

_____ So a

priest walks into a bar, ….. that's all I got.

_____

_____

_____

_____

_____

_____

_____

_____

_____

_____

_____

_____

_____

_____

_____ Who in their right mind would buy

a book like this?

_____

_____

_____

_____

_____

_____

_____

_____

_____

_____

_____

_____ I hope you at least got free

shipping and handling with this book

_____

_____

_____

_____

_____

_____

_____

_____

_____

_____

_____ Can blind people see their

dreams?

_____ How do bankruptcy

attorneys make any money?

_____

_____

_____

_____

_____

_____

_____

_____

_____

_____

_____

_____

_____

_____

_____

_____

_____Why do they say the alarm

clock goes 'off' when in reality, it turned

on?

_____

_____

_____

_____

_____

_____

_____

_____

_____

_____Aren

't all mysteries unsolved in the beginning.

Isn't that why they are called a mystery?

_____

_____

_____

_____

_____

_____ wow, you have reached page

53 _____

_____

_____

_____

_____

_____ Just to recap, You won't

find any good use for this book.

_____

_____

_____

_____

.

_____

_____

_____

_____ well, maybe you can prop

up a table leg with it

_____

_____

_____

_____

_____

_____

_____

_____

_____

_____

_____ Are you actually

writing notes in this book?

_____

_____

_____

_____

_____

____ HA HA HA HA HA

_____

_____

_____ Pull my finger

_____

_____

_____

_____

_____

_____

_____

_____

_____

_____ If you

pamper a cow and give it everything it

wants, does it give you spoiled milk?

_____

_____ Now

is the time you should go outside and

actually do something.

_____

_____

_____

_____

_____

_____

_Find Gregory Hudson Books on facebook

and like me. Please

the author of this book actually does

have a serious side

—

_____ It's the left side, look closely

_____ How many days did it take

you to get this far in his book?

_____

_____

_____

_____

_____

_____

_____

_____

_____ Do mermaids lay eggs?

_____ Write down your

random thoughts here

_____

_____

_____

_____

_____

_____

_____

_____

lets get our doodle on

And more doodle

This doodle page is stupid

How many geese does it take to fill up

the insides of a volkswagon?

_____

_____

_____

_____

_____

_____

_____

_____

Smile, it's really not that bad

_____

_____

_____

_____

Can you draw at least 30 happy faces on this page?

What percentage of the world is

covered with milk chocolate?

_____

_____

_____

_____

_____

_____

_____ MMmmmm chocolate

You know, when you say the world 'Smile'

you actually smile

_____

_____

_____

_____

_____

_____

_____

_____

SMILE

_____

_____

_____

_____

When you say 'Boo' you pucker your lips,

and who doesn't like kisses?

_____

_____

_____

_____

_____

_____

_____

_____

_____

_____

_____

_____

_____

the absolute worst thing about this book is?

_____

_____

_____

_____ que the music, make it loud

_____

_____

_____

_____

_____

_____

_____ If people from Poland are called

Poles, why aren't people from Holand called

Holes?

_____

_____

_____

_____

_____

_____

_____

_____

_____

_____

_____

_____

_____ If you are

cured from amnesia, can you remember that

you had no memory?

_____

_____

_____

_____

_____

_____

_____

_____

_____

_____

_____

_____

_____

Why do you say 'after dark' when it's

actually 'After Light' ?

_____

_____

_____

_____

_____

_____

_____

_____ the

best day of my life was ....

_____

_____

_____

_____

_____

_____

_____

_____

_____

_____

_____

_____ Does this

book make you happy?

_____

_____

_____

_____

_____

_____

_____

_____

_____

_____ or is it just a waste of

time?

_____

_____

_____

_____

_____

_____

_____

_____ grape fruit doesn't look like grapes and

besides, aren't grapes already a fruit?

_____

_____

_____

_____

_____

_____

_____

_____Are all lady bugs female?

_____

_____

_____

_____

_____

_____

_____

_____

_____

_____

_____ When someone

describes them self as being indecisive, are

they decisive or indecisive?

_____

_____

_____

_____

_____ More doodle for your noodle __

Doodle here

doodle ooodle doo doo

dipity doodle time

wooo hooooo

_____ Are you still here?

_____

_____

_____

_____

happy days are here again

say what??????

me me me

Whatcha

thinking?_____

_____

_____

_____

_____

_____

_____

Don't do it, ... too late

You said it, I didn't

What If?

This is

amazing_____

_____

_____

_____

_____ simply amazing _____

_____

_____

_____

Now it the time for precise decisions

Yes, I mean You!!

and You!!

What does a dog think?

How often do you (fill in the blank)

_____

now answer your own question

_____

This page is made just for you

so is this page

my my my what did you do with all of

those blank

pages?_____

_____

_____

_____

_____

Gregory Hudson Books on Facebook

I can't believe you made it to the very last

page

Yep this is it, the last page

This Book belongs to

_____

If lost, please return it to this address

_____

_____

_____

_____

_____

Made in the USA
Middletown, DE
30 April 2023